EXPERT@ EXCEL VBA PROGRAMMING

A Step By Step Guide to Learn and Master VBA Programming to Get Ahead @ Work, Business and Personal Finances

Disclaimer Notice

Please note the information contained within this document is for educational and entertainment purposes only. All effort has been executed to present accurate, up to date, and reliable, complete information. No warranties of any kind are declared or implied. Readers acknowledge that the author is not engaging in the rendering of legal, financial, medical or professional advice. The content within this book has been derived from various sources. Please consult a licensed professional before attempting any techniques outlined in this book.

By reading this document, the reader agrees that under no circumstances is the author responsible for any losses, direct or indirect, which are incurred as a result of the use of information contained within this document, including, but not limited to, — errors, omissions, or inaccuracies.

Contents

INTRODUCTION

I want to thank you for choosing this book, 'Expert@Excel VBA Programming: A Step By Step Guide to Learn and Master VBA Programming to get Ahead @ Work, Business and Personal Finances.'

VBA (Visual Basic for Applications) is a tool that empowers you to perform tasks you never thought possible in a fraction of the time that it takes to perform the task by hand. For example, you can add new toolbars, create custom reports, and perform special kinds of data analysis. When you write a VBA program, you become the expert in your industry since you become someone who can get a job done quickly.

If you want to learn VBA programming, you have come to the right place. This book will guide you throughout your journey. Over the course of the book, you will gather information on what VBA is and how it functions. When you write code, you must know what data types to use and how you can build modules and functions. This book will teach you everything you need to know about VBA.

To make the learning interesting, there are some exercises provided at the end of some chapters. You should try to write the code yourself before you look at the solutions provided to you at the end of the book. Remember that practice will make you better at coding. You will make errors, and these errors will help you become a better programmer.

Over the course of this book, you will gather information on the different data types used in VBA, the conditional statements, loops, arrays and other important information about VBA. You will also gather information on how you should handle errors when you code. Use the exercises in this book as practice. Once you can write these programs without any errors, you can build larger programs.

Thank you for purchasing this book. I hope you gather all the information you are looking for.

CHAPTER ONE
INTRODUCTION TO VBA

Visual Basic for Applications (VBA) is a programming language that is compatible with most Microsoft Office products, including Excel. In other words, you can use VBA to develop programs in Excel. These programs will make Excel operate accurately and very fast.

What Can You Do With VBA?

Most people use Excel for a million different reasons. Here are a few examples:

- Forecasting and budgeting
- Analyzing data
- Developing diagrams and charts using data
- Creating lists
- Creating forms and invoices

This list is endless, but I am sure you get the idea. In other words, you can use Excel to perform a variety of tasks, and I am sure you are reading this book because you have a set of expectations. If you want to automate the functions of Excel, you should use VBA.

For example, you may want to create a program that will help you import some data or numbers and then format that data to print a report. Once you develop the code, you can execute the macro using a command or a button. This will ensure that Excel performs the task in a few seconds or minutes.

Common Uses of VBA

You must understand why you want to use VBA. You must ensure that you can take some time out of your busy schedule to sit down and write a VBA code. You must understand the different tasks you can use VBA for. You cannot use VBA to perform your chores, but you can use it to make some tasks easier for you. This section covers some tasks that you can perform with VBA.

Automating Documents

Most people do not like to prepare documents, and if these documents contain the same information, they will not want to work on that document. You can use the Excel Add-in called Mail Merge to automate letters, but this is not an option to use when you want to write individual letters or documents. In such situations, you can use a VBA code to create a form that will include the common information. You can include check boxes that VBA will use to write the document for you.

Word processing is not the only task you can automate using VBA. You can also automate the spreadsheet, and there are numerous programs you can create for the same. For example, you can extract information or data from the Internet into a spreadsheet by clicking a button; therefore, you can limit the time you spend on simply copying the data from the web and pasting it according to the required format in your Excel worksheet.

Customizing Application Interfaces

There are times when the features of an application will bug you, and you can turn off those features, but that is not an option if you want to use that feature in your work. Instead of disabling that feature, you can use VBA to create a new feature, which has all the functions that you need. For instance, instead of using conditional formatting every time you need to make changes in a worksheet, you can write a VBA code to do that for you.

It is easy to change the interface of an application, so it works better for you. You can customize toolbars or menu systems, and can also move some elements around in the interface to make it look presentable. Additionally, you can use multiple interfaces and use a VBA code to shift between those interfaces.

One of the most common applications of VBA is to perform a variety of calculations. You can create different equations and graphs using the data you obtain. There are times when you will need to make changes to the data so you can perform some calculations on it. If you find that an equation is complicated, you can use VBA to simplify the process. You can also use iterative functions to perform a calculation.

Sometimes, the number that you create using a calculation does not mean much — it is just a number until someone makes a decision. Some decisions are easy to make, yet repetitive. Smart applications save you more time for playing that game of Solitaire.

Adding New Application Features

Most vendors or developers never use the applications they build; therefore, they never update the code for their application. You can add new features to the application using VBA codes and work on developing an application. When you develop applications that complete some of your work in a few minutes, you will impress your boss and colleagues. This is an added advantage to using VBA.

Chapter Two
The IDE

VBA is a visual programming environment. That is, you see how your program will look before you run it. Its editor is very visual, using various windows to make your programming experience easy and manageable. You will notice slight differences in the appearance of the editor when you use it with Vista as compared to older versions of Windows. No matter which Office product and version of Windows you use, the editor has essentially the same appearance (and some small differences), the same menu items, and the same functionality.

An IDE (Integrated Development Environment) is an editor, just like your word processor, spreadsheet, or database form. Just as application, editors have special features that make them especially useful for working with data; an IDE is a programming editor with special features that make it useful for writing instructions that the application should follow. These instructions are procedural codes — a set of steps. The figure below shows you the IDE Window in Excel:

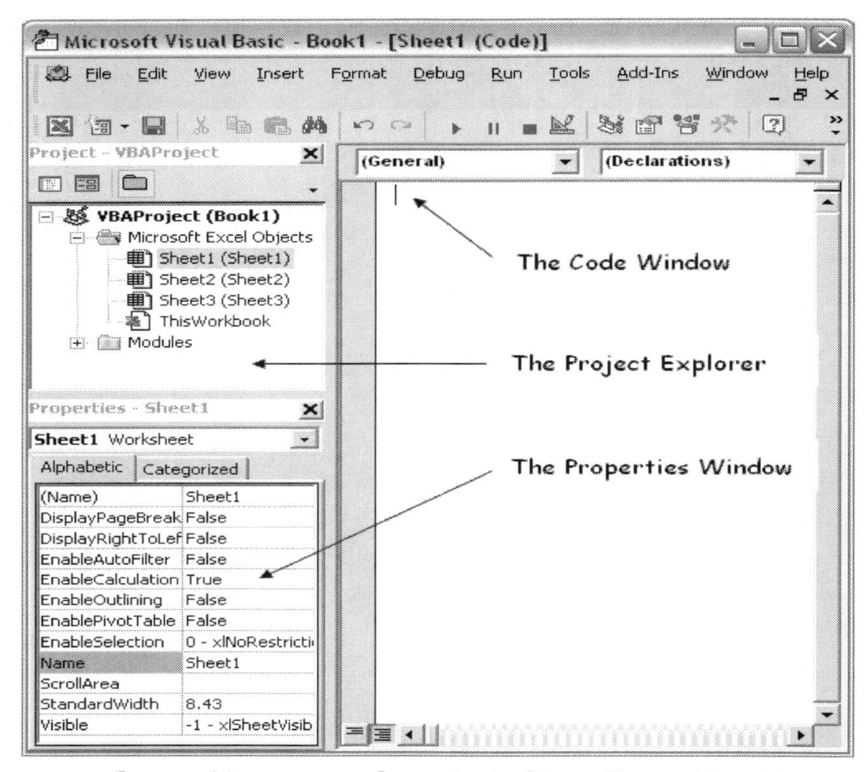

(https://www.google.co.in/url?sa=i&rct=j&q=&esrc=s&source=images&cd=&cad=rja&uact=8&ved=2ahUKEwjDrZTGofrdAhUIEnIKHWGVCVMQjRx6BAgBEAU&url=http%3A%2F%2Fwww.databison.com%2Fhow-to-write-a-macro-in-excel%2F&psig=AOvVaw0XYs9S9qRneDdPgmz6Bmld&ust=1539218405542672)

The VBA IDE consists of a menu system, toolbars, a Project Explorer window, a Properties window, and a Code window. Below is a summary of what each Window contains.

Project Explorer

This window contains a list of the items in your project, which contains all the document elements in a single file. Your application exists within a file that appears in the Project Explorer window.

Properties

Whenever you select an object, the Properties window tells you about it. For example, this window tells you whether the object is blue or whether it has words on it.

Code

Eventually, you must write some code to make your application work. This window contains the special words that tell your application what to do. Think of it as a place to write a specialized to-do list.

Looking at the VBA Toolbox

You will not have to write code for every task in VBA. The IDE also supports forms, just like the forms that you use to perform other tasks. In this case, you decide what appears on the form, and how the form acts when the user works with it. To make it easier to create forms, VBA provides the Toolbox, which contains controls used to create forms.

Each Toolbox button performs a unique task. For example, when you click one button, a text box may appear on the screen but, if you click another button, a mathematical operation may take place.

Starting the Visual Basic Editor

How you start the Visual Basic Editor depends on the application that you are using. Newer versions of Office use a different approach than older versions.

Step 1: Go to Option "View" on the toolbar.
Step 2: In the drop-down list, select "Record Macro."
Step 3: The interface will open, and you can begin typing the code for the worksheet you are in.

Using Project Explorer

Project Explorer appears in the Project Explorer window. You use it to interact with the objects that make up a project. A project is an individual file used to hold your program, or at least pieces of it. The project resides within the Office document that you are using, so, when you open the Office document, you also open the project. See Chapter 3 for a description of how projects and programs interact. Project Explorer works much like how the left pane of Windows Explorer does.

The objects listed in Project Explorer depend on the kind of application that you are working with. For example, if you are working with Word, you see documents and document templates. Likewise, if you are working with Excel, you see worksheets and workbooks. No matter what kind of application you work with, the way that you use Project Explorer is the same.

A project can contain forms, modules, and class modules. Here is a description of these special objects:

- **Forms**: Contain user interface elements and help you interact with the user.
- **Modules**: Contain the nonvisual code for your application. For example, you can use a module to store a special calculation.
- **Class modules**: Contain new objects that you want to build. You can use a class module to create a new data type.

Working with Special Entries

Sometimes you see a special entry in Project Explorer. For example, when you work with a Word document, you might see a References folder, which contains any references that the Word document makes. Normally, it contains a list of templates that the document relies upon for formatting.

In many cases, you cannot modify the objects in the special folders. This is the case with the References folder used by Word document objects. The References folder is there for information only. To modify the referenced template, you need to find its object in Project Explorer. We will not discuss these concepts in the book since you do not work with these often.

Using the Properties Window

Most of the objects that you click in the VBA IDE have properties that describe the object in some way. The following sections provide details about the Properties window.

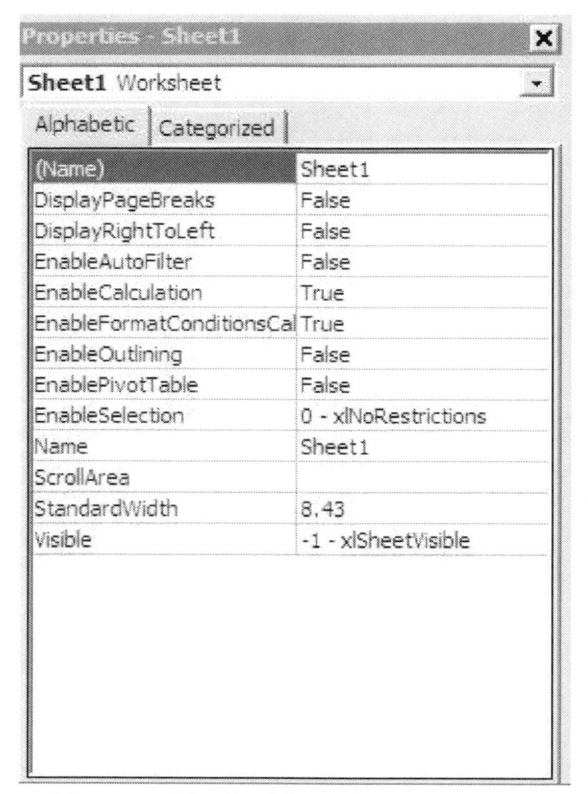

(http://www.affordsol.be/vba-prog-1-3-editor-properties.htm)

Understanding Property Types

A property needs to describe the object. When you look at an object, you naturally assume some information about the object – its color, type or any other specification. Likewise, VBA object properties have specific types. One of the most common property types is text. The caption property of a form is text. The text appears at the top of the form when the user opens it. Another common property type is a logic, or Boolean, value.

Getting Help with Properties

Do not expect to memorize every property for every object that VBA applications can create. Not even the gurus can do that. To determine what a property will do for your application, just highlight the property and press F1, and, in most cases, VBA displays a Help window like the image below.

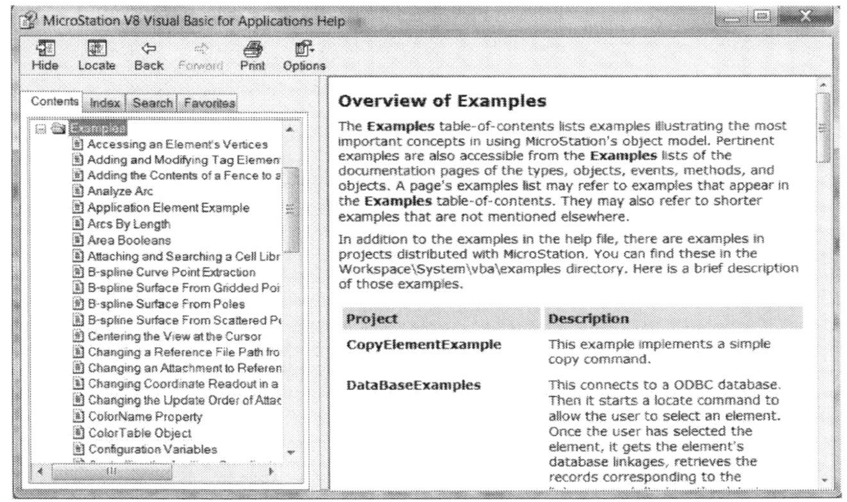

(http://www.la-solutions.co.uk/content/V8/MVBA/MVBA-Tips.htm)

Using the Code Window

The Code window is where you write your application code. It works like any other editor that you have used, except that you type according to the syntax.

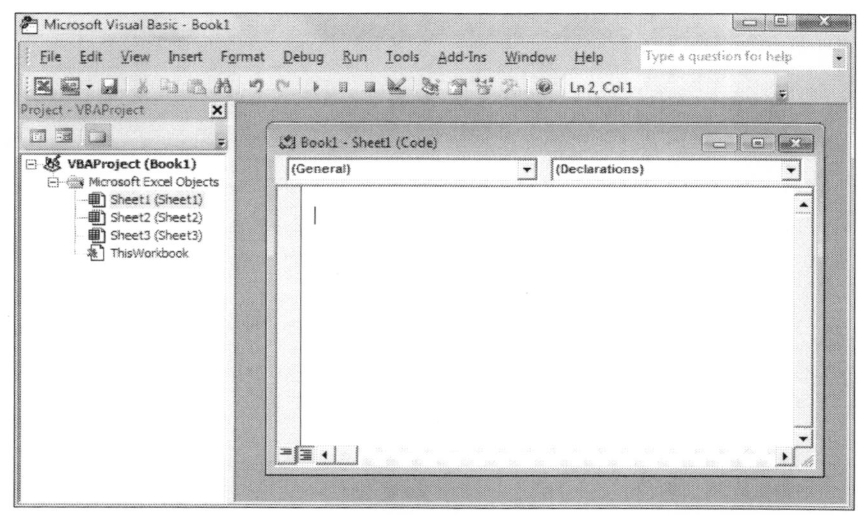

(http://www.homeandlearn.org/the_excel_vba_editor.html)

Notice that the Project Explorer window and the Properties window are gone — you can display them again by using the View -> Project Explorer and View ->Properties Window commands.

Opening an Existing Code Window

Sometimes, you will not be able to complete an application and need to work on it later. To open an existing Code window, find the module that you want to open in Project Explorer. Double-click the module entry, and the IDE displays the code within it with your code loaded. The Code window also appears when you perform different tasks.

Creating a New Code Window

When you start a new module within an existing document or template, open a new Code window by using either the Insert -> Module or Insert -> Class Module command. After you save this module or class module, it appears in Project

Explorer with the other modules in your project.

It is easier to execute one line of code at a time to understand where you may have made an error. You can do this by using the Immediate Window. This window normally appears at the bottom of the IDE, and it will not contain any information until you type something in it.

Most developers spend their days using the Immediate window to check their applications for errors. You can use the Immediate window to ask VBA about the value of a variable, for example. To try this feature, type String1 = "Hello World" in the Immediate window and then press Enter. Now type '? String1' and then press Enter. You asked VBA to create a variable named String1 and assign it a value of Hello World. You can use the '?' operator to check the value assigned to the variable String1.

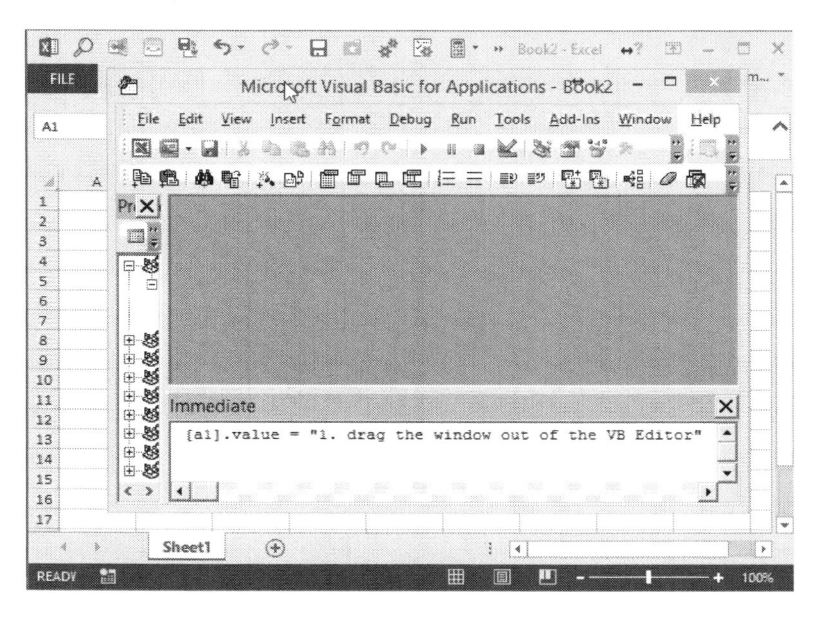

(https://www.excelcampus.com/vba/vba-immediate-window-excel/)

CHAPTER THREE
WRITING A PROGRAM

In the previous chapter, we looked at how one can work with the Integrated Development Environment (IDE). In this chapter, we will learn to write a one-line code. This chapter shows you how to move from the immediate window into the Code window. The Code window is where you create programs of a lasting nature - the kind that you can use to perform the same task more than once. Since it takes time for anybody to write a code, it makes sense to only write code to perform repetitive tasks. You can also look for code available online, and make changes to that code to use for your application. This will help you save time.

The help files that come with VBA contain a lot of code that you can use in several ways. Microsoft knows that some developers want to use the code, so it tries to make the samples as flexible as possible.

Deciding What to Do

Whenever you decide to create a program, start with a plan. The plan that you use does not have to be very complicated, but you do need to think about these questions:

- What will the program do?
- How will the program accomplish its task?
- When will the program run?
- Who will use the program?
- Why is the program important?

Professional developers use several complex and hair-raising methods to answer these questions. You work on much smaller programs, and you can normally answer the questions quite easily. Do not make this more complicated than you need to. You might answer the first question by saying, for example, that the program will count the number of words in a document.

The reason that you want to go through this planning process is to ensure that you have thought about the program you want to create. It is easier to answer the questions before you write any code than to fix the code later.

Steps to Write Your Program

Design the Program

When you know what your code should be about, you can use different methods to design the flow of the program. It is best to write a pseudo code since it will help you to think clearly about what you want from your program. You also do not have to worry about the errors in the pseudo code yet. Let us look at the code to saying hello.

```
Sub Hello()

MsgBox Prompt := “Hello World!”

‘Printing the message “Hello World

End Sub
```

Implement the Code

Now that you have your pseudo code, open the Code Window and start writing the VBA Code. The Code Window will come with the following information: You should write your code in between the lines "*Sub() .... End Sub()*."

Test the Code

You should run the code and check if there are any bugs in your code. If an error box pops up, select the option to debug the code. The debugger highlights the errant section of the code in red. If you are unsure of why that error has come up, copy that line of code and paste it in the bottom section of the Code Window with a question mark ahead of it. The debugger will tell you which part of the code is incorrect.

CHAPTER FOUR
PARTS OF A PROGRAM

You should follow a syntax and a structure when you want to write a code in VBA to help the debugger understand what the point of your code is. This chapter formalizes the meaning for each structural element.

Defining the Parts of a Program

A program is the highest level of physical structure. It contains everything needed to perform a given task. A program can cross module, class module, and form boundaries. The concept of a program comes from the earliest use of computers. A program acts as a container for the code used to implement a set of features required by the operating system or the user. Some people have a hard time understanding what a program is because modern software packages often define the term incorrectly. You are not creating a new program when you create a new project. A VBA project can actually contain a number of VBA programs.

Programming Blocks

A VBA program consists of building blocks. In fact, because programming is abstract, people tend to use physical examples to explain how things work. You still need to know about the abstract elements of VBA programming, or else you cannot write a program. This section explains the basic constructs of VBA programming. Every VBA code has the following elements:

- **Project**: The project acts as a container for the modules, class modules, and forms for a file. Excel users normally see just one project for the file that they have open.
- **Module, class module, and forms**: These three elements act as containers for main programming elements, such as class descriptions and procedures. A single project can have multiple modules, class modules, and forms in it; however, each of these elements requires a unique name.
- **Function and Sub**: The Function and Sub elements hold individual lines of code (also called statements). A Function returns a value to the caller, but a Sub does not. Microsoft Office provides access to code functionality through the Sub, not through the Function. Consequently, you must always provide access to your VBA program by using a Sub.
- **Statement**: Many people call an individual line of code a statement.

Using the Macro Recorder

The Macro Recorder lets you record keystrokes and actions that you perform as a VBA program. You can use it to record complete tasks, such as setting up a document, or for partial tasks, such as highlighting text and giving it certain attributes. The Macro Recorder can help you perform the following tasks:

- Create a macro based on your actions.
- Discover how Word performs certain tasks.
- Decide how to break your program into tasks.
- Help you create the basis for a more complex program.

The Macro Recorder is not a complete solution for your VBA needs. For example, you cannot use the Macro Recorder to create interactive programs without extra coding. The same holds true for programs that must change based on user input, the environment, or the data you are manipulating. All these tasks require you to add more code; however, it is a good starting point for many structured programming tasks. You can get the basics down quickly using the Macro Recorder and then make changes as needed.

- Start the Macro Recorder.
- Perform all the steps that you normally perform to accomplish a task.
- Stop the Macro Recorder.
- Save the macro when the Office application prompts you.
- Optionally, open the resulting macro and make any required changes.

Using Subs

A Sub is the easiest method of packaging code, and it is the only packaging method that appears in the Macro dialog box. Consequently, the one place where you always use a Sub is the main entry point for a program, unless the program is a utility that you use only for programming purposes. A second way to use a Sub is to perform a task and not receive a direct return value. You can use a Sub to display an informational message. A Sub can modify information in several ways; it just cannot return a value — only a Function can do that. You can use arguments as one method for modifying information by using a Sub. A second method relies on global variables. Many VBA users also use the Sub as a means of breaking up the code.

Instead of creating code that goes on for miles and miles, using several Subs can break up the code into page-sized pieces. Using this method makes the code a lot easier to read.

```
Sub FirstCode()

    Dim FormatCell As Integer

    FormatCell = ActiveCell.Value

    If FormatCell < 20 Then

        Call SecondCode

    End If

End Sub
```

(https://www.homeandlearn.org/excel_vba_subroutines.html)

Using Functions

You might not see a use for the Function after spending some time working with the Sub, but not every problem is a screw that requires the use of a screwdriver or a nail in search of a hammer. You must identify where you can use a sub and where you can use a function. For example, you always use a Sub when you want to access a program code from within the host application, and you always use a Function when you want to perform a calculation which will return a result.

A Function always returns a value, which makes it different from a Sub. For this reason, you can write functions that contain code that you plan to repeat a lot within a program. To process a list of names, you might create a Function to process each name individually and then call that Function once for each name. The Function can provide the processed information as a return value. In Chapter 5, I describe how to create repeating code using structures such as Do...Until.

You can also use a Function for public code that you do not want to list in the Macro dialog box. You normally do not see a Function listed in the Macro dialog box — this dialog box usually lists only Subs.

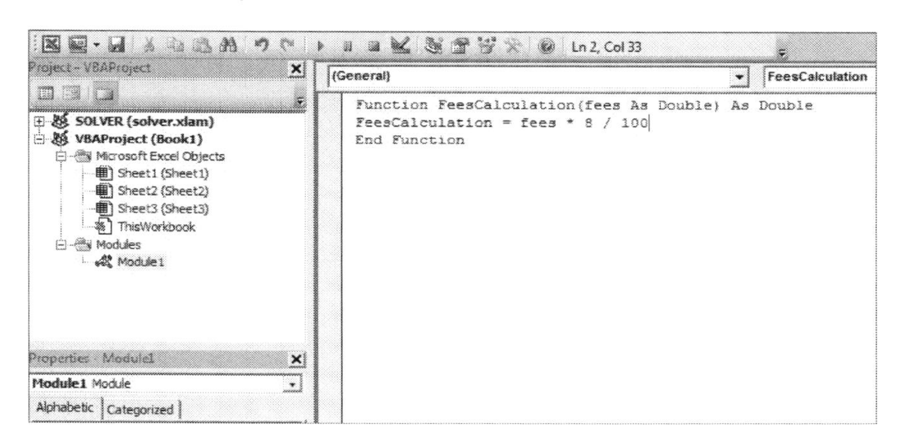

(https://www.thewindowsclub.com/create-custom-excel-functions)

Comments

It is important to write comments in your code to help other users understand the purpose of the code.

Writing Basic Comments

Comments can take several forms. The pseudo-code comment is the first kind of comment that everyone writes because it is the kind of comment that is most natural to use. Developers quickly move on to adding documentation comments, such as who wrote the program, or when it was originally written, and a list of updates made to the code. Some developers move on to better comments at this point.

One of the more important comments that you can add to your code is why you chose to write the program in a certain way. Simply saying that the code performs a specific task is not enough because you can usually perform the same task in several different ways. Telling why you made certain choices could reduce mistakes during code updates, and serve as reasons to perform updates later when your coding technique improves.

As a good programmer, you should also include mistakes that you make in the code as comments if you think that someone else might make the same mistake.

Knowing When to Use Comments

Use comments wherever and whenever you think that you need them. You might think that comments are difficult to type and include only one or two paltry comments for each program that you write. You are correct — writing good comments can be time-consuming and can be difficult because writing them makes you think yet again about the code. When you do not have enough comments in your code, you will find it difficult to update that program. You may also have to start writing the code from scratch because you do not know what your code is all about.

Writing Good Comments

A good comment is one that you can understand. Do not use fancy terms — write everything in plain terms that you can understand. If you think you want to explain a certain line of code, feel free to do it. You can also write comments against every line of code since that will help an amateur understand your train of thought.

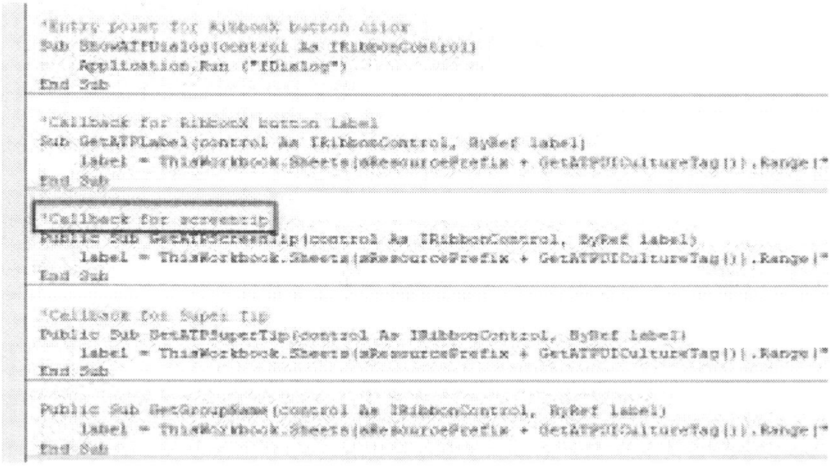

```
'Entry point for RibbonX button click
Sub ShowATPDialog(control As IRibbonControl)
    Application.Run ("fDialog")
End Sub

'Callback for RibbonX button label
Sub GetATPLabel(control As IRibbonControl, ByRef label)
    label = ThisWorkbook.Sheets(sResourcePrefix + GetATPUICultureTag()).Range("
End Sub

'Callback for screentip
Public Sub GetATPScreenTip(control As IRibbonControl, ByRef label)
    label = ThisWorkbook.Sheets(sResourcePrefix + GetATPUICultureTag()).Range("
End Sub

'Callback for Super Tip
Public Sub GetATPSuperTip(control As IRibbonControl, ByRef label)
    label = ThisWorkbook.Sheets(sResourcePrefix + GetATPUICultureTag()).Range("
End Sub

Public Sub GetGroupName(control As IRibbonControl, ByRef label)
    label = ThisWorkbook.Sheets(sResourcePrefix + GetATPUICultureTag()).Range("
End Sub
```

(https://spreadsheeto.com/vba-comments/)

CHAPTER FIVE
DATA TYPES

A data type is a method of defining data to make it easier to work within a program. The computer still sees the data as a series of bits, but VBA works with different data types in different ways. The computer can see the binary value, 1000001b, but it does not do anything special with that value. VBA can see this binary value as the number 65, or the letter A, depending on the data type that you assign to the value. The data type is important in understanding the value and working with it. Using a data type also ensures that the program follows certain rules; otherwise, the data could become corrupted because the program could mishandle it.

Although a variable, in general, is simply a box for storing data, you can think of these data types as special boxes for storing specific kinds of data. Just as you would use a hatbox to store a hat and not a car engine, you use these special box types to store kinds of data. For example, you use a string to hold text, not logical (true/false) values. VBA supports several standard data types, including Byte, Boolean, Integer, Long, Currency, Decimal, Single, Double, Date, String, Object, and Variant. In addition to using the defined data types, you can create user-defined data types so that you can mark the information as needed for your program. A user-defined data type gives you the power to extend the VBA interpretation of data. (The computer still looks at the data as binary information.) Each of the data type descriptions that follows has a different purpose, and you can work with the data type in a variety of ways.

Using Strings for Text

The first data type that I discuss in this chapter is one that you have already seen in the message box examples: the string. When you create a message box, you use a string as input. The string is the most useful data type in VBA. This chapter only introduces strings. The next chapter provides information on how you can manipulate strings in VBA.

Understanding Strings

Programmers often use fancy terms for things that the average person easily recognizes. A string is a sequence of characters. The characters are not always printable, but can include control characters that determine how the text appears onscreen. A string can also include special characters, such as punctuation, or even special features, such as a circumflex or an umlaut. Although a string can contain all these elements, the main content of a string is always text.

Adding Strings Together with + or &

Sometimes you will want to concatenate two or more strings to make a longer string. Concatenation is the process of adding strings together. For example, you might want to add a person's first name to their last name to create their full name. Often, you need to take information from more than one place and join it together to create a new kind of information.

Using Character Codes

Strings can contain several elements. In previous examples, I show you strings that contain control character constants such as vbCrLf. This constant contains two control characters: a carriage return and a line feed. The carriage return sends the cursor back to the beginning of the line; the line feed places the cursor on the next line. The result of using both control characters together is the same as pressing Enter on the keyboard. Strings can also use a special function, Chr, to create special characters. You can combine this function with the Character Map utility to produce any character that you need for your program.

Using Numbers for Calculations

Numbers form the basis for a lot of the information computers store. You use numbers to perform tasks in a spreadsheet, to express quantities in a database, and to show the current page in a document. Programs also use numbers to count things such as loops, to determine the position of items such as characters in a string, and to check the truth-value of a statement. Finally, VBA uses numbers in myriad ways, such as determining which character to display onscreen or how to interact with your code.

Understanding the Numeric Types

You look at numbers as a single entity — a number is simply a number. The computer views numbers in several different ways. The reason for this diversity of viewpoints is that the processor works with different kinds of numbers in different places: one for integer values (those without a decimal point) and another for floating-point values (those with a decimal point). The four basic number types include:

- **Integer**: This is a number without a decimal. An integer can hold any whole number, such as 5, but not a number with a decimal, such as 5.0. Although these two numbers are the same, the first is an integer and the second is not.

- **Real**: A real number is one that contains a decimal point. The decimal portion does not have to contain a value. The number 5.0 is a perfectly acceptable real number. VBA stores a real number in a different format when compared to the format of an integer.
- **Currency**: Financial calculations usually require special accuracy. Even a small error can cause problems. The currency numeric type stores numbers with extreme precision, but at an equally large cost in both processing time and memory use.
- **Decimal**: Computers normally store information by using a base 2 or binary format. There are times when you will need to use numbers with a base 10 in some calculations and these numbers are called decimals. Small errors can occur when converting from one numbering system to the other and accumulate to create huge errors. The decimal numeric system stores numbers in a simulated base 10 format, which eliminates many computing errors. This system, however, requires more memory and processing time than any other numeric type.

Using Boolean Values to Make Decisions

The Boolean type is the easiest to use and understand. This type is used to indicate yes or no, true or false and on or off. You can use this type to work with any two-state information. This operator is used to represent data variables and values that are diametrically opposed.

Working with Operators

Operators determine how VBA works with two variables and what result it produces. The examples in this chapter use operators to add numbers and concatenate (add) strings. In both cases, your code uses the + operator to perform the task; however, the result differs. When you are using numbers, the result is a summation, such as 1 + 2 = 3. When you are using strings, the result is a concatenation, such as Hello + World = Hello World.

VBA groups operators into four areas:

- **Arithmetic**: Operators that perform math operations, such as addition (+), subtraction (-), division (/), and multiplication (*).
- **Comparison**: Operators such as less than (<), greater than (>), and equal (=) that compare two values and produce a Boolean result.
- **Concatenation**: Operators such as & and + that are used to add two strings together.
- **Logical**: Operators such as Not, And, Or, and Xor that are used to perform Boolean operations on two variables.

Exercises

- Write a program to add two numbers.
- Write a program to concatenate two strings.

Chapter Six
Decision-Making Statements

Only a few programs use all the statements in the program file all the time. You might want the program to perform one task when you click Yes and another task when you click No. The statements for both tasks appear in the code, but the program executes only one set of statements. To control program execution, the developer adds special statements — such as the If...Then statement. This statement defines which function needs to be performed if the condition is true and what to perform otherwise. You might think that letting the computer decide which task to execute would cause the developer to lose control of the program. The developer has not lost control of the program, because the decision-making process is predefined as part of the program design.

If...Then Statement

Most programs require decision-making code. When you need to make the same decision every time that you perform a task, and the outcome of the decision is always the same, then making the decision is something that you can tell VBA to do for you by using the If...Then statement. Decision-making code has several benefits:

- **Consistency**: The decision is made by using the same criteria and in the same manner every time.
- **Speed**: A computer can make static decisions faster

than humans can; however, the decision must be the same every time, and the decision must have the same answer set every time.

- **Complexity**: Requesting that the computer make static decisions can reduce program complexity. Fewer decisions translate into ease of use for most people.

Example:

```
Public Sub IfThenTest()

‘ Create a variable for the selected text.

Dim TestText As String

‘ Get the current selection.

TestText = ActiveWindow.Selection.Text

‘ Test the selection for “Hello.”

If TestText = “Hello” Then

‘ Modify the selected text to show it’s correct.

TestText = “Correct!” + vbCrLf + “Hello”

End If
```

If...Then...Else statement

The If...Then...Else statement makes one of two choices. If the expression controlling the statement is true, VBA executes the first set of statements. On the other hand, if the expression is false, VBA executes the second set of statements.

If...Then...ElseIf statement

When making multiple comparisons, you can use the If...Then...ElseIf statement to make the code easier to read. Using this format can also reduce the number of decisions that VBA must make, which ensures that your code runs as quickly as possible.

```
Sub If_Test_2()

    Dim MyNumber As Integer

    MyNumber = 11

    If MyNumber = 10 Then
        MsgBox "Number = 10"

    ElseIf MyNumber = 11 Then
         MsgBox "Number = 11"

    End If

End Sub
```

(http://www.homeandlearn.org/else_else_if.html)

Using the IIf function

You might need to decide in a single line of code instead of the three lines (minimum) that other decision-making techniques require. The IIf function is a good choice when you need to make simple and concise decisions in your program. It has the advantage of providing decision-making capability in a single line of code.

Exercises

- Write a program to check if a number is prime.
- Write a program to illustrate the use of the IIf function.

Chapter Seven
Loops

Many tasks that you perform require more than one check, change, or data manipulation. You do not change just one entry in a worksheet; you change all the affected entries. Likewise, you do not change just one word in a document; you might change all occurrences based on certain criteria. Databases require multiple changes for almost any task.

Loops provide a method for performing tasks for more than one time. You can use loops to save code-writing time. Simply write the code to perform the repetitive task once and then tell VBA to perform the task multiple times. When using loops, you decide how the code determines when to stop. You can tell the loop to execute a specific number of times, or to continue executing until the program meets a certain condition.

Do While...Loop Statement

A Do While...Loop statement keeps performing a task until a certain condition is true. The loop checks the expression first and then executes the code within the structure if the expression is true. You use this loop to perform processing zero or more times. A Do While...Loop works especially well if you cannot determine the number of times that the loop should execute when you design your program.

Do...Loop While Statement

The Do...Loop While statement works the same as the Do While...Loop statement. The difference is that this statement always executes once because the expression used to verify a need to loop appears at the end of the structure. Even if the expression is false, this statement still executes at least one time. You can use this statement when you want to ensure that a task is always completed at least one time.

Do Until...Loop Statement

The Do Until...Loop statement continues processing information until the expression is false. You can view the Do While...Loop statement, as a loop that continues while a task is incomplete. The Do Until...Loop statement continues until the task is finished. The subtle difference between the two statements points out something interesting – they rely on your perspective of the task to complete. These two statement types are completely interchangeable. The big difference is how you define the expression used to signal the end of the looping sequence.

Do...Loop Until Statement

The Do...Loop Until statement is the counterpart of the Do Until...Loop statement. This statement examines the expression at the end of the loop, so it always executes at least once even if the expression is false.

For...Next Statement

The For...Next statement is very handy for performing a task a specific number of times. If you can determine how many times to do something in advance, this is the best looping option to use because there is less chance of creating an infinite loop. You can create absurdly large loops, but they eventually end.

For Each...Next Statement

The For Each...Next statement is like the For...Next statement in operation; however, this statement does not rely on an external counter. The statement uses an object index as a counter. The advantage of using this statement is that you do not have to figure out how many times to perform the loop — the object provides this information. The disadvantage of using this statement is that you lose a little control over how the loop executes because the counter is no longer under your control.

Exercises

- Write a program to print the Fibonacci series.
- Write a program to use the For Each...Next Statement.

CHAPTER EIGHT
ARRAYS

Arrays provide a way for your programs to store more than one item in a single container. Think of the array as a large box with a bunch of small boxes inside. Each small box can store a single value. You decide how many small boxes the array can hold when you create the array. Use arrays when you need to store several related items of the same data type.

Structured Storage

An array is a list of items. When you write a list of tasks to perform for the day, you create an array. The piece of paper is a single container that holds several strings, each of which is a task that you must perform. Likewise, you can create a single piece of paper in your VBA program — an array — and use that array to hold multiple items. You can define arrays by using several techniques; however, all these techniques use the same basic approach.

Example:

```
' Tell VBA to start all arrays at 0

Option Base 0

Public Sub SingleDimension()

' Define an output string
```

```
Dim Output As String
' Define a variant to hold individual strings
Dim IndividualString As Variant
' Define the array of strings
Dim StringArray(5) As String
' Fill each array element with information
StringArray(0) = "This"
StringArray(1) = "Is"
StringArray(2) = "An"
StringArray(3) = "Array"
StringArray(4) = "Of"
StringArray(5) = "Strings"
' Use the For Each...Next statement to get each array
' element and place it in a string
For Each IndividualString In StringArray
' Create a single output string with the array
' array elements
Output = Output + IndividualString + " "
Next
' Display the result
MsgBox Trim(Output), _
```

```
vbInformation Or vbOKOnly, _
"Array Content"
End Sub
```

Notice that the code begins with an Option Base 0 statement. This statement tells VBA whether you want to start counting array elements at 0 or 1. The default setting is 0. Most programming languages use 0 as the starting point, which is why Microsoft made 0 the default for VBA. The older versions of Visual Basic (including VBA) use 1 as the starting point. When you want to ensure that your program works in every environment, include the Option Base statement.

Because the array begins at 0 and not at 1, you can store six items in an array that is defined as having five elements. The number that you include in the declaration is always the top element number of the array and not the actual number of elements.

Array Types

You can classify arrays in several ways. The first method is by the kind of data that the array holds. A String array is different from an Integer array. An array always keeps the array data type unique. Using a Variant data type lets you mix data types within an array. You should use this technique carefully because it can lead to bugs that are difficult to debug.

A second method is to define the number of array dimensions. A dimension is the number of directions in which the array holds information. A simple list is a single-dimensional array. A table that consists of rows and columns is a two-dimensional array. You can create arrays with any number of dimensions.

Example: Adding an Element to an Array

Dim a As Range

Dim arr As Variant 'Just a Variant variable (i.e. don't pre-define it as an array)

For Each a In Range.Cells

If IsEmpty(arr) Then

arr = Array(a.value) 'Make the Variant an array with a single element

Else

ReDim Preserve arr(UBound(arr) + 1) 'Add next array element

arr(UBound(arr)) = a.value 'Assign the array element

End If

Next

CHAPTER NINE
WORKING WITH EXCEL WORKBOOKS AND WORKSHEETS

The Workbook Collection

The Workbook collection contains a list of all the workbooks that are open at any given time. From this list, you can select a single Workbook object to use in your program. The Workbook object contains general information about the file, such as its name and location. You can also use the Workbook object to access any other major object in the document, which includes all Worksheet objects and standalone Chart objects.

Example:

Public Sub WorkbookDemo()

' Holds the output data

Dim Output As String

' Get the test workbook

Dim ActiveWorkbook As Workbook

Set ActiveWorkbook =

Application.Workbooks("ExcelObjects.xls")

' Get the workbook name and location

Output = "Name: " + ActiveWorkbook.Name + vbCrLf + _

"Full Name: " + ActiveWorkbook.FullName + vbCrLf + _

"Path: " + ActiveWorkbook.Path + vbCrLf + vbCrLf

' Holds the current sheet

Dim CurrSheet As Worksheet

' Look for every sheet

Output = "Worksheet List:" + vbCrLf

For Each CurrSheet In ActiveWorkbook.Worksheets

Output = Output + CurrSheet.Name + vbCrLf

Next

' Holds the current chart

Dim CurrChart As Chart

' Look for every chart

Output = Output + vbCrLf + "Chart List:" + vbCrLf

For Each CurrChart In ActiveWorkbook.Charts

Output = Output + CurrChart.Name + vbCrLf

Next

' Display the output

MsgBox Output, vbInformation Or vbOKOnly, "Object List"

```
End Sub
```

The code begins by using the Application.Workbooks collection to retrieve a single Workbook object. Notice that you must use the full name of the Excel file, including the file extension, as an index into the collection. The resulting Workbook object contains the name and path information for the document. It also contains settings, such as the summary information. You can use this object to control windows and add new main elements, such as a worksheet.

After the code has access to the workbook, it uses the ActiveWorkbook object to access the list of worksheets. As usual, the code relies on a For Each...Next statement. You can also use an index to access individual worksheets in your code. The Worksheet, ActiveWorksheet, contains properties and methods for manipulating any data that the worksheet contains, including embedded objects, such as charts or even pictures. Every worksheet appears in the ActiveWorkbook object list by its object name (not the friendly name that you give it), so you can access them without using the worksheets collection.

Unlike worksheets, only independent charts appear as part of ActiveWorkbook. You use the same technique to access a Chart object as a Worksheet object. The only difference is that you must use the Charts collection. Note that chart names appear in the list of objects presented by ActiveWorkbook, so you can also access the chart directly as an object without using the Charts collection.

The Worksheet Collection

The Sheets collection is the easiest method for accessing

worksheets in many situations. You do not have to drill down through the Excel object hierarchy to find the worksheet that you want. Accessing the worksheets at the top of the hierarchy means that you do not have the objects that exist at lower levels available either, so this technique is a tradeoff.

You can use the Sheets collection to access all kinds of sheets, not just worksheets. Any standalone Chart objects also appear in this collection. Look at the example in the earlier section "Using the Workbooks collection," and you see that it treats charts and worksheets as separate objects.

Example:

```
Public Sub ListSheets()

' An individual entry

Dim ThisEntry As Variant

' Holds the output data

Dim Output As String

' Get the current number of worksheets

Output = "Sheet Count: " + _

CStr(Application.Sheets.Count)

' List each worksheet in turn

For Each ThisEntry In Application.Sheets

' Verify there is a sheet to work with

If ThisEntry.Type = XlSheetType.xlWorksheet Then

Output = Output + vbCrLf + ThisEntry.Name
```

```
End If

Next

' Display the result

MsgBox Output, _

vbInformation or vbOKOnly, _

"Worksheet List"

End Sub
```

The code for this example begins by creating a Variant to hold the various sheet types. If you use a Worksheet or a Chart object, the code fails because the Sheets enumeration can return any valid type — not just one valid type. The problem with using a Variant is that VBA cannot provide balloon help or automatic completion. You must be sure that you type the correct method and property names without the usual help.

After the code creates the required variables, it gets the number of sheets in the workbook. This number includes all the worksheets and charts and not just the worksheets.

A For Each...Next loop retrieves each sheet in turn. Notice how the code uses an If...Then statement to compare the Variant type with the XlSheetType.xlWorksheet constant. Using this technique lets you separate the worksheets from other Sheets Collection Types as needed.

Charts Collection

One of the most useful purposes of the Charts collection is building a custom chart whenever you need one. The advantage of creating uncommon charts by using code is that they take up less space. In addition, you can create variations on a theme without a lot of work.

Example:

```
Public Sub BuildChart()

' Create a new chart

Dim NewChart As Chart

Set NewChart = Charts.Add(After:=Charts(Charts.Count))

' Change the name

NewChart.Name = "Added Chart"

' Create a series for the chart

Dim TheSeries As Series

NewChart.SeriesCollection.Add _

Source:=Worksheets("My Data Sheet").Range("A$3:B$8")

Set TheSeries = NewChart.SeriesCollection(1)

' Change the chart type

TheSeries.ChartType = xl3DPie

' Change the series title

TheSeries.Name = "Data from My Data Sheet"

' Perform some data formatting

With TheSeries
```

```
.HasDataLabels = True
.DataLabels.ShowValue = True
.DataLabels.Font.Italic = True
.DataLabels.Font.Size = 14
End With
' Modify the chart's legend
With NewChart
.HasLegend = True
.Legend.Font.Size = 14
End With
' Modify the 3-D view
With NewChart
.Pie3DGroup.FirstSliceAngle = 90
.Elevation = 45
End With
' Format the chart title
NewChart.ChartTitle.Font.Bold = True
NewChart.ChartTitle.Font.Size = 18
NewChart.ChartTitle.Format.Line.DashStyle _
= msoLineSolid
NewChart.ChartTitle.Format.Line.Style = msoLineSingle
```

```
NewChart.ChartTitle.Format.Line.Weight = 2
‘ Compute the optimal plot area size
Dim Size As Integer
If NewChart.PlotArea.Height > NewChart.PlotArea.Width
Then
Size = NewChart.PlotArea.Width
Else
Size = NewChart.PlotArea.Height
End If
‘ Reduce the plot area by 10%
Size = Size - (Size * 0.1)
‘ Format the plot area
With NewChart.PlotArea
.Interior.Color = RGB(255, 255, 255)
.Border.LineStyle = XlLineStyle.xlLineStyleNone
.Height = Size
.Width = Size
.Top = 75
.Left = 100
End With
‘ Format the labels
```

```
Dim ChartLabels As DataLabel

Set ChartLabels = TheSeries.DataLabels(0)

ChartLabels.Position = xlLabelPositionOutsideEnd

End Sub
```

The code begins by creating a new chart. This chart should appear as the last chart in the workbook, but not necessarily as the last item in the workbook. Any worksheets that appear after the existing last chart also appear after the new chart. The NewChart.Name property changes the name that appears on the tab at the bottom of the chart — the property does not change the chart title.

The chart is blank at this point. To display any data, you must add at least one data series to the chart. A pie chart uses only one data series at a time, but other charts can support (or might even require) multiple data series. For example, a bubble chart requires multiple data series. Consequently, the next task that the code performs is creating a data series based on the My Data Sheet worksheet supplied with the example. Notice that the code cannot set TheSeries equal to the output of the Add method in this case, so it uses an extra step to get the new series from the SeriesCollection collection.

Notice that the Range property contains two columns of information. When you are working with Excel 2007, the first column defines the XValues property for the chart. The XValues property determines the entries in the legend for a pie chart. On the other hand, these values appear at the bottom of the display for a bar chart. In both cases, you want to display the labels onscreen so that you can see their effect on the overall display area.

User Forms

User forms are dialog boxes that allow a user to enter data comfortably. The data entered can be controlled easily. This section will help you build a simple form and add information in Excel.

Step 1: Open the VBA Window by clicking on Alt + F11. Now, navigate to the "Insert" option and choose "User Form." When you select this option, you obtain the following screen.

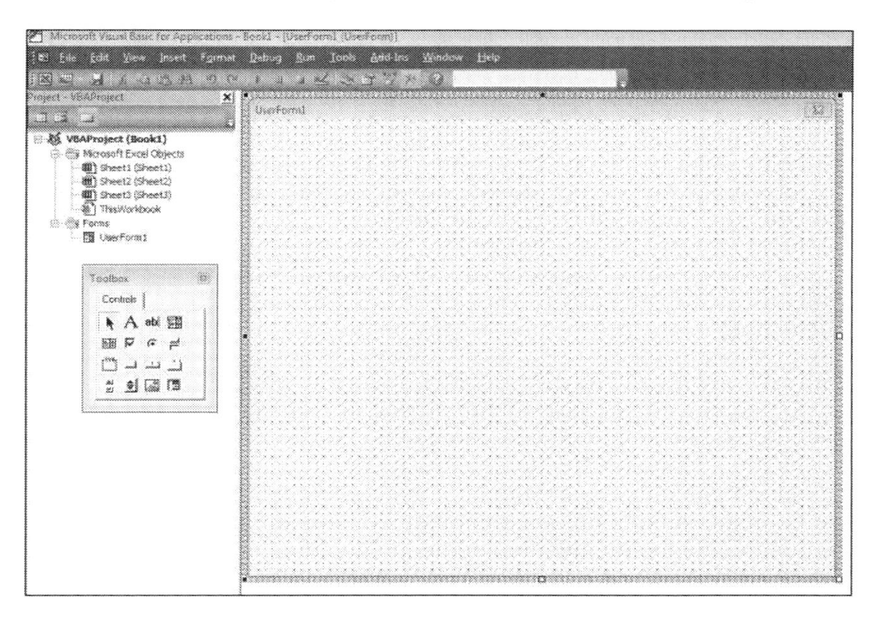

(https://www.tutorialspoint.com/vba/vba_userforms.htm)

Step 2: Design a form using the controls available to you in the window.

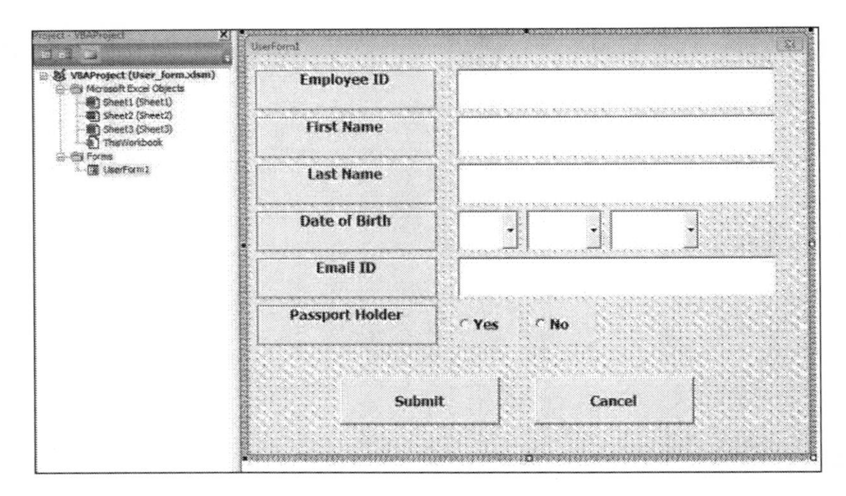

(https://www.tutorialspoint.com/vba/vba_userforms.htm)

Step 3: When you add controls, you should remember to name those controls. The Caption allows you to define the words that should appear on the screen. The name of the control defines the variable that is used when writing the VBA code.

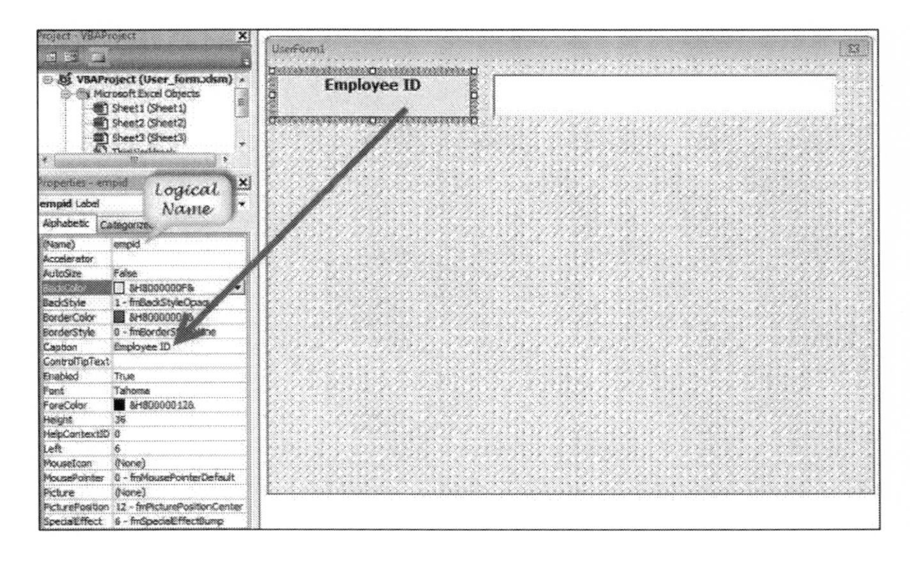

Step 4: Once you have created the form, begin to write the code.

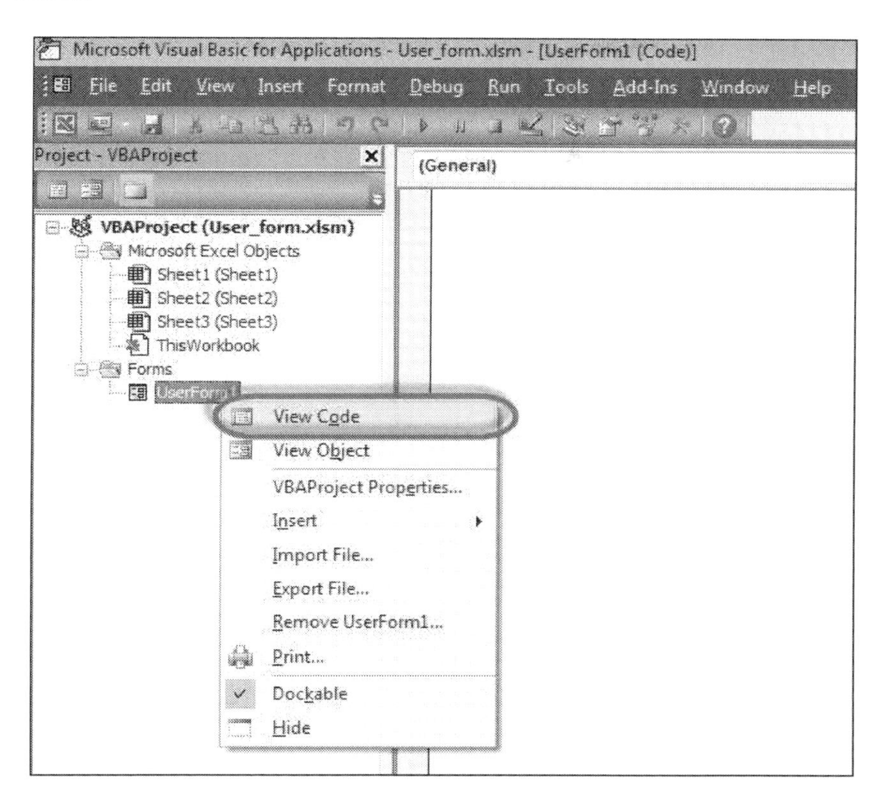

(https://www.tutorialspoint.com/vba/vba_userforms.htm)

Step 5: Select the option of Userform from the dropdown and write the code for every radio button in the screen. You can also write a code to close the user form once the user has answered the questions.

Step 6: Execute the form by selecting the "Run" button.

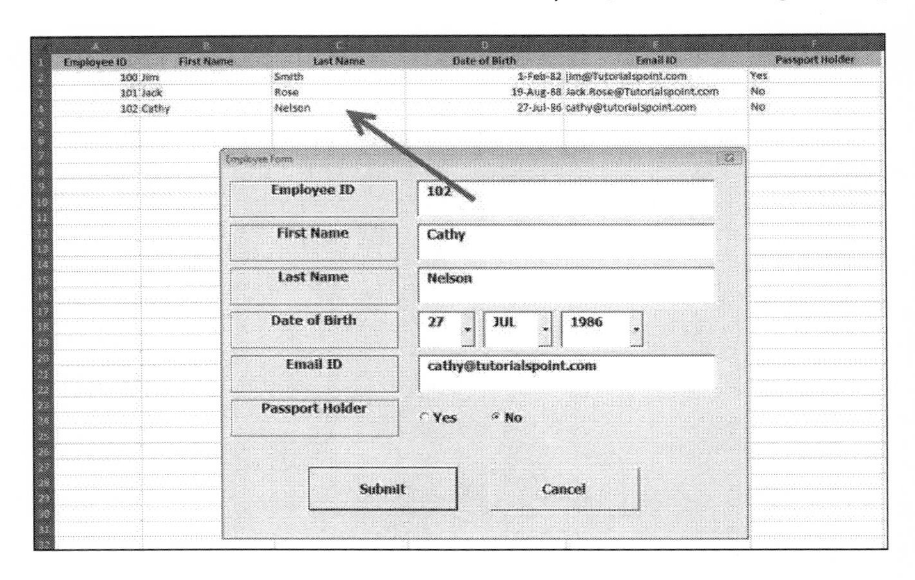

(https://www.tutorialspoint.com/vba/vba_userforms.htm)

CHAPTER TEN
HOW TO REDIRECT THE FLOW

You might run into situations where the existing program flow does not work, and you must disrupt it to move somewhere else in the code. The GoTo statement provides a means of redirecting program flow. Used carefully, the GoTo statement can help you overcome specific programming problems. Unfortunately, the GoTo statement has caused more problems (such as creating hard-to-understand code and hiding programming errors) than any other programming statement because it has a great potential for misuse. Novice programmers find it easier to use the GoTo statement to overcome programming errors rather than to fix these problems. Always use the GoTo statement with extreme care. Designing your code to flow well before you write it and fixing errors when you find them, are both easier than reading code with misused GoTo statements.

Using the GoTo Statement Correctly

The GoTo statement provides the essential service of helping you redirect program flow. Before you use the GoTo statement, ask yourself whether there are some other means of performing the redirection, such as using a loop. If there is not any other way to perform the programming task efficiently, using a GoTo statement is acceptable.

- **Loops**: Never use a GoTo statement as a loop replacement. The statements used for loops signal others about your intent. In addition, standard loop statements contain features that keep bugs, such as endless loops, to a minimum.

- **Exits**: Avoid using a GoTo statement as a means of exiting a program. You can always use the End statement for that task.
- **Program flow problems**: If you detect problems with the flow of your program, check your pseudo-code and design documents again. Make sure that you implement the design correctly. The design might require change as well. Do not assume that the design is correct, especially if this is the first attempt.

Chapter Eleven
Error Handling

Syntax errors are the easiest errors to avoid, but are also some of the hardest errors to find. A syntax error can include a spelling mistake, misuse of punctuation, or misuse of a language element. When you forget to include an End If for an If...Then statement, it is a syntax error.

Typos are common syntax errors. They are especially hard to find when you make them in variable names. For example, VBA views MySpecialVariable and MySpecialVaraible as two different variables, but you might miss the typing error. Adding Option Explicit to the beginning of every module, form, and the class module that you create eases this problem. You can rely on VBA to find most variable typos when you add this simple statement to your code. In fact, this statement should become a standard part of every program that you create.

You can easily miss some of the subtle aids in locating syntax errors if you do not view carefully enough the tasks that the Integrated Development Environment (IDE) performs. VBA displays the balloon help shown in the figure only when it recognizes the function name that you type. When you do not see the balloon help, it is a cue that VBA does not recognize the function name, and that you need to look at your code.

Unfortunately, this feature works only where VBA normally displays balloon help — it does not work when you type property names.

Understanding Compile Errors

VBA uses the compiler to look for errors that prevents the program from running properly. You might create an If...Then statement and not include the corresponding End If statement. The compiler runs constantly, so VBA finds some mistakes almost immediately after you make them.

VBA uses the compiler to find many of the syntax errors that you make and displays an error message. You can try this feature - open a new project, create a Sub (the name is not important), and type MsgBox(). Then press Enter. VBA displays a message box stating that it was expecting an equal to sign (=). When you use parentheses after MsgBox, VBA expects that you want to include a result variable to hold the result, such as MyResult = MsgBox("My Prompt"). As mentioned earlier, the debugger highlights the error in red.

Understanding Run-time Errors

A run-time error happens when something outside your program is incorrect. A disk access request can fail, or you can type in the wrong information. Your VBA code is correct, but the program still fails because of this external error. Run-time errors are the reason many large companies, such as Microsoft, run beta programs. (A beta program is a vendor-sponsored method of getting a program before its developers have finished it for testing.)

Understanding Semantic Errors

A particularly difficult error to find and understand is the semantic error, which happens when the VBA code and logic are correct but the meaning behind the code is not what you intended. For example, you could use a Do...Until loop in place of a Do...While loop. Even if the code is correct and you use the correct logic, the code does not produce the result that you expected because the meaning of a Do...Until loop is different from the meaning of a Do...While loop.

The meaning that you assign to your code has to match the words that you use to write the code. Just as a good book uses precise terms, a good program relies on precise statements to ensure that VBA understands what you want to do. The best way to avoid semantic errors is to plan your application carefully, use pseudo-code to "pre-write" the design, and then convert the pseudo-code to VBA code.

Chapter Twelve
VBA and Text Files

It is easy to work with text files since they are an easy way to store and read information. You can use them to save any settings for VBA add-ins. You can also extract information from databases into text files (.txt format) if you have a large dataset. This chapter covers some of the functions you can perform using text files. Before we look at the functions, we should understand some terminology. This is because these terms are not used in regular VBA codes.

Terminology

For Input

When you open the text file using this command, you are indicating to the compiler that you want to extract some information from a text file. You cannot modify any information in the text file when you use this command to open the file.

For Output

When you open a text file using this command, you tell the compiler that you want to modify or create the file. You cannot pull or extract any information from the text file when you use this command.

FreeFile

The command is used to tell the compiler to use

information from a file that is not in use. This is similar to the reference function that you use to open workbooks. When you use FreeFile, the compiler will return the reference number of the text file.

For Append

This command will add a new text to the bottom of the text file that you are using.

Write

This command allows you to write a text that is enclosed within quotation marks.

Print

This command writes a line in the text file without using quotation marks.

Examples

To Create a New Text File

```
Sub TextFile_Create()

'Purpose is to create a new text file

Dim TextFile As Integer

Dim FilePath As String

'The file path to the new text file

 FilePath = "C:\Users\User\File.txt"

'Determine the next file number that the compiler can
```

open

```
TextFile = FreeFile
'Open the text file
Open FilePath For Output As TextFile
'Write some lines of text
Print #TextFile, "Hello World!"
Print #TextFile, "I am using VBA to create this file."
Print #TextFile, "Have a nice day!"
'Save & Close Text File
Close TextFile
End Sub
```

Extract Data From a Text File

```
Sub TextFile_PullData()
'Move data from the text file into a string variable
Dim TextFile As Integer
Dim FilePath As String
Dim FileContent As String
'The file to use as the source
FilePath = " C:\Users\User\File.txt "
'Determine the next file number that the compiler can open
```

```
  TextFile = FreeFile
  Open FilePath For Input As TextFile
'Store file content inside a variable
  FileContent = Input(LOF(TextFile), TextFile)
'Report Out Text File Contents
  MsgBox FileContent
'Close Text File
  Close TextFile
End Sub
```

Exercises

- Write a program to modify the information in a text file.

CHAPTER THIRTEEN SOLUTIONS

Sum of Two Numbers

```
Private Sub Calculate_Click ()

Dim a As Integer

Dim b As Integer

Dim c As Integer

a = Val(`TextBox1.Text`)

b = Val(`TextBox2.Text`)

c = a + b

MsgBox (c)

End Sub
```

Concatenate Two Strings

```
Sub ConcatenateStrings()

Dim str1 As String, str2 As String

str1 = "Captain"

str2 = "America"

'returns "Captain America":
```

```
MsgBox str1 & str2
MsgBox str1 & " " & str2
'returns "Captain America":
MsgBox str1 & " " & str2 & " in Australia"
'returns "Captain America in Australia":
End Sub
```

Prime Number

```
Function IsPrime(Num As Double) As Boolean
Dim i As Double
If Int(Num / 2) = (Num / 2) Then
Exit Function
Else
For i = 3 To Sqr(Num) Step 2
If Int(Num / i) = (Num / i) Then
Exit Function
End If
Next i
End If
IsPrime = True
End Function
```

IIf Function

```
‘Test if a Supplied Integer is Positive or Negative

Dim testVal As Integer

Dim sign1 As String

Dim sign2 As String

‘First call to IIf function. The test value is negative:

testVal = -2

sign1 = IIf( testVal < 0, "negative," "positive" )

‘Sign1 is now equal to "negative"

‘Second call to IIf function. The test value is positive:

testVal = 8

sign2 = IIf( testVal < 0, "negative," "positive" )

‘Sign2 is now equal to "positive"
```

Fibonacci Series

```
Private Sub Command1_Click()

Dim x, g, n, i, sum As Integer

n = Val(Text1.Text)

x = 0

y = 1

Print x
```

```
Print y
For i = 3 To n
sum = x + y
Print sum
x = y
y = sum
y = sum
Next i
End Sub
```

For Each...Next Statement

```
Sub Unhide_First_Sheet_Exit_For()
'Unhides the first sheet that contains a specific phrase
'in the sheet name, then exits the loop.
Dim ws As Worksheet
  For Each ws In ActiveWorkbook.Worksheets
  'Find the sheet that starts with the word "Report"
If Left(ws.Name, 6) = "Report" Then
  ws.Visible = xlSheetVisible
  'Exit the loop after the first sheet is found
Exit For
```

```
End If
Next ws
End Sub
```

Modify a Text File

```
Sub TextFile_FindReplace()
'Modify the information in a text file using find and replace
Dim TextFile As Integer
Dim FilePath As String
Dim FileContent As String
'File Path of Text File
  FilePath = " C:\Users\User\File.txt "
'Determine the next file number available for use by the FileOpen function
  TextFile = FreeFile
'Open the text file in a Read State
  Open FilePath For Input As TextFile
'Store file content inside a variable
  FileContent = Input(LOF(TextFile), TextFile)
'Clost Text File
  Close TextFile
```

'Find/Replace

FileContent = Replace(FileContent, "Goodbye," "Cheers")

'Determine the next file number available for use by the FileOpen function

TextFile = FreeFile

'Open the text file in a Write State

Open FilePath For Output As TextFile

'Write New Text data to file

Print #TextFile, FileContent

'Close Text File

Close TextFile

End Sub

CONCLUSION

Thank you for purchasing this book.

Most organizations have begun to use VBA to automate some of their processes in Excel. You can copy and paste information or create a pivot in Excel using VBA. If you want to learn VBA coding to improve processes at your workplace, you can use this book as your guide.

Over the course of this book, you will gather information on the different data types used in VBA, the conditional statements, loops, arrays and other important information about VBA. You will also gather information on how you should handle errors when you code. Use the exercises in this book as practice. Once you can write these programs without any errors, you can build larger programs.

You should remember that experts also make errors when they build programs or applications; therefore, you should not beat yourself up if you make mistakes. Instead, take some time to understand what the error is, and what can be done to fix it. You should constantly practice to master programming in VBA.

I hope you gather all the information you are looking for. I hope you can automate some or all the processes that you work on in your company, and impress your colleagues and bosses!

SOURCES

https://www.excel-pratique.com/en/vba/introduction.php

http://www.easyexcelvba.com/introduction.html

https://www.tutorialspoint.com/excel_vba_online_training/excel_vba_introduction.asp

https://www.thespreadsheetguru.com/getting-started-with-vba/

https://www.tutorialspoint.com/vba/vba_strings.htm

https://www.excel-easy.com/vba/string-manipulation.html

https://www.guru99.com/vba-data-types-variables-constant.html

https://corporatefinanceinstitute.com/resources/excel/study/vba-variables-dim/

https://powerspreadsheets.com/vba-data-types/

https://www.tutorialspoint.com/vba/vba_loops.htm

https://www.excel-easy.com/vba/loop.html

https://www.excelfunctions.net/vba-loops.html

https://powerspreadsheets.com/excel-vba-loops/

https://www.excelfunctions.net/vba-conditional-statements.html

https://analysistabs.com/excel-vba/conditional-statements/

https://www.techonthenet.com/excel/formulas/if_then.php

http://www.cpearson.com/excel/errorhandling.htm

https://excelmacromastery.com/vba-error-handling/

https://docs.microsoft.com/en-us/dotnet/visual-basic/language-reference/statements/on-error-statement

Made in the USA
Columbia, SC
08 January 2019